First published in 2022 by Fiercely Independent Books,
in partnership with whitefox publishing

www.wearewhitefox.com

All photographs © Unsplash.
Photographers credited in order of appearance:
John O'Nolan; Clay Banks; Saad Chaudhry; Yousef Espanioly; Jeff W;
Bao Sabrina; Evie S; Nahil Naseer; Sime Basioli; Tabitha Turner; Zac Ong;
Daniela Beleva; Mio Ito; Alex Cao; Magic Bowls; Enache Georgiana;
Laura Adai; Vino Li; Alex Perez; Sime Basioli; Annie Spratt; Freestocks;
Wonderlane; Dapo Oni; Taylor Van Riper;
Rinck Content Studio; Mathew Schwartz

ISBN 978-1-915036-34-6
Also available as an ebook
ISBN 978-1-915036-35-3

Designed and illustrated by Karen Lilje / Koki Design
Project management by whitefox
Printed and bound by CPI Group (UK) Ltd, Croydon CR0 4YY

THE LITTLE BOOK OF

Self-Love

*50 Practical Ways to Heal a
Broken Heart and Raise Your Vibration*

JADE JAEGER

*This book was my way
of stitching back together
a broken heart.*

INTRODUCTION

I wanted to create something humble, simple and beautiful. Something that would be of service to others who are hurting, and who don't know how to begin to mend their own hearts.

This little book is 50 practical things I did to manifest love in myself and towards myself in order to heal myself. I have filled it with witchcraft, rituals, self-care practices, tips and recipes all designed to make yourself feel loved. By consciously raising your vibration (see page 11) you can create abundance and happiness.

It is broken down into easily digestible points so you can try everything yourself. You can open the book at any page and it will tell you what you have to do in that moment.

Heartbreak is universal and non-discriminatory. It doesn't care about age, race, class or gender. I am not an expert or a psychologist (although I have been to plenty). I am a human being writing for other human beings going through similar experiences. I know what worked for me, and I hope these things will work for you too.

They cultivate routines to give you joy. Our day-to-day lives are made up of small daily rituals so it is important to find beauty and love in these tasks.

Each of these practical exercises can be used to bring back balance and open your heart each time you lose your way.

As soon as you start actively practising these things, magic will happen. Your pain will transform into a deep expression of love for your friends and family, and, most importantly, you.

After a while, you will do the exercises as an expression of pure love for yourself, and because it is natural. When that happens you will finally know how to take care of yourself.

We are responsible for our own happiness!

HOW IT WORKS

◇

My suggestion is to read through the book once and try the exercises one at a time. Repeat the ones you like, and begin to cultivate a morning ritual. Or in the case of first aid, just open the book and let an exercise be chosen for you.

A NOTE ABOUT PAIN

We spend so much of our lives running from pain. We medicate, disassociate and distract ourselves from this wretched feeling.

When I sat in a puddle on my shower floor the day I found out my marriage of twelve years was over, it occurred to me that instead of allowing the emotion to swallow me, I would run towards it and feel every part of it. I wouldn't waste that pain anymore – I would use it to grow and to evolve and to transform.

It would be my biggest teacher and catalyst for change and transformation. I surrendered to it and let it happen to me. At its own pace.

What was born out of that pain was this book.

Everything in life is vibration, everything is energy. ALBERT EINSTEIN

If all of life is vibration, it follows that your emotions and your thoughts vibrate as well, along with your words. The word itself carries the power of creation, the vibratory gateway to unleash the potency of the universe.

I came to find what Albert Einstein already knew 65 years ago. Love is the highest vibration there is and love has no limits.

Love is always the answer to any question.

A NOTE ABOUT SPELL CASTING

There are a few things you must do before casting a spell. Firstly, you must practise good spiritual hygiene – clean both yourself and your space. Secondly, you must create sacred space by smudging (see page 46) the room or area where you will be casting magic and make sure you will not be disturbed. Thirdly, you must meditate for five minutes beforehand and visualise white light surrounding your body and glowing out of you like a protective orb.

LASTLY, REMEMBER THE RULE OF THREE. WHATEVER YOU PUT INTO THE UNIVERSE COMES BACK TIMES THREE, SO SEND LOVE AND LIGHT IN WHATEVER SPELLS YOU DO.

Start with just five minutes a day of breathing in for four seconds and out for four seconds.

THE RIGHT VIBRATION

What is high vibration?

Simply put, it is a life full of love, positivity, compassion and peace. The higher your vibration, the more capable you are of manifesting the life you desire.

What is low vibration?

Basically, negativity, fear, resentment, hate, jealousy and anger all reside in the low-vibe frequency.

Apart from it feeling really crappy to live this way, it is also how illness manifests and nobody wants that.

How do I get high vibration?

Read the book and try the activities!

How to begin a spiritual practice?

Start reading, listen to podcasts, join a spiritual or meditation group. These are all great ways to begin. Keep an open mind and always use both critical thinking and your intuition combined.

Critical thinking is logical thinking and intuition is that non-verbal part of you that just knows.

Swearing

The vibration of swear words emits negative energy. It sounds and feels ugly. Remember words are your wand!

Doing stuff that goes against your values

When we do things that go against who we are at a soul level, we are going against our truth. When we are not true to ourselves, we are not aligned with a higher good, which totally lowers vibration.

Watching porn or violent movies

Ultimately TV is a form of conditioning. There are lots of subliminal messages on TV that program us to believe certain things about ourselves and life that are not truthful. TV influences your world view at an unconscious level. According to research, porn and violent movies can erode the prefrontal cortex, an area of the brain critical for impulse control. They also damage the dopamine reward system.

Mistreating yourself, other people, animals or the planet

Any sort of hurtful, selfish and unconscious behaviour is low vibe. When you understand that we are all interconnected and from one energy source, you realise that this behaviour hurts yourself, both karmically and otherwise.

Ummm, I still struggle with swearing, but I do it far less than I used to. Sometimes I lose all my words and the F word forms in my mouth before I can stop it.

If you stay away or limit these activities you will find more joy and love in your life. That's it.

Mindless activities

Social media and browsing the internet for no real purpose. Doing repetitive things out of habit that don't make you feel alive or happy. Working a job you hate. Playing violent video games. Reading gossip magazines, engaging in drama.

Addictive behaviour

Drinking alcohol or taking drugs, or any addictive behaviour like gambling, sex or shopping. Anything that is mood- or mind-altering will leave you feeling low after the temporary buzz wears off. Or dead. Or with an STD.

Eating crappy food

Anything chemically enhanced, genetically modified or highly processed foods, or animal products. Be aware of where your food comes from and if it aligns with your beliefs. You are responsible for what goes in your body and you are responsible for finding out how that product got on the shelves. Research! Remember that if it is not aligned with truth, love, connection and compassion it is going to lower your vibration.

Gossiping

It's like consuming fast food, it feels good while you're doing it then you feel sick. Mostly with yourself.

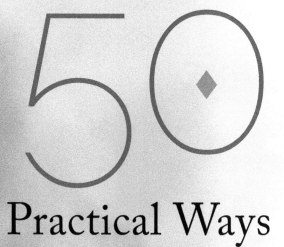

50

Practical Ways

TO HEAL A BROKEN HEART AND RAISE YOUR VIBRATION

1

Breathe

*Did you know that
the first thing we do
when we are in a panic
is stop breathing?*

BREATHING RITUAL

Lie on your back with your hands on your belly.

Bring your feet close to your bum and let your knees fall apart.

Inhale for four seconds and exhale for four seconds.

When you are good and calm begin to visualise a white light filling every cell in your body as you inhale and as you exhale let all the negative stuff out like it's black smoke leaving your body.

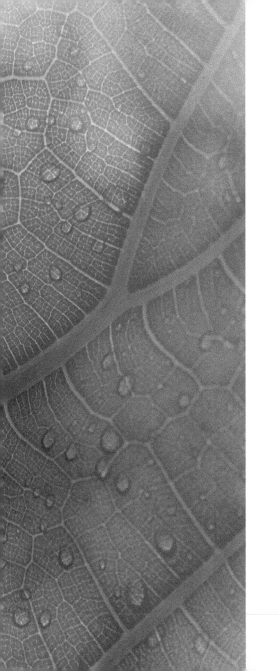

2 Bathe

I run myself a love
bath a couple of times
a week. Use rose petals
or dried lavender or
even chamomile tea in
the water depending
on your mood and
what you would like to
manifest for yourself.

LOVE BATHS

Run a love bath, light a candle, put some crystals in the water and rose or lavender oil and a cup of epsom salts.

Soak for 20 minutes and chill TFO.

Make a cup of rose or chamomile tea and sip it while you're in there.

After you're done wrap yourself in a warm fluffy towel and put on your comfiest pjs.

Ahhhhhhhhh.

Ingredients

Seven drops essential oil, lavender or rose

½ cup epsom salts

Handful of flower petals or dried fragrant herbs like
chamomile, lavender or rose

Candle

Herbal tea such as rose, lavender or chamomile are
best for setting the mood

Moon water (see page 127)

Crystals, such as rose quartz

Incense (rose if you have it otherwise any incense
that evokes a loving feeling or smells great)

Method

Run your bath and add your moon water to it as it's
running. Light your incense, add your essential oil,
petals or herbs, epsom salts and any crystals like rose
quartz to the bath.

Next put a few drops of essential oil on the candle
and sweep in an upwards motion towards you. Use a
sharp knife to etch into the candle 'I love you [insert
name]' and then light it and dim the lights.

Brew your tea as the bath runs and think about your
heart chakra (see page 87) glowing green and bright in
your chest.

Take your tea into the bath and begin by taking long deep inhales and exhales, counting slowly to four each time.

On the inhale imagine white light filling your body. When you exhale imagine black smoke and all the negative energy leaving your body in a thick cloud.

When your mind is very still begin to imagine how your life would look filled with love. Imagine your body, your clothes, your home. Go into minute detail. This is your ultimate life you are imagining so don't limit yourself!

When you have completed the ritual, get out and cover yourself in a warm fluffy towel and rub into your body oil or cream that smells sweet, preferably rose but really anything you love will do.

Stand naked in front of your mirror and say, 'I love you [insert name]. I really really love you.'

IF YOU DON'T HAVE A BATH, PUT DROPS OF ESSENTIAL OIL ON THE FLOOR OF THE SHOWER AND THE STEAM WILL ACT AS AN INFUSER. SIT ON THE FLOOR OF THE SHOWER AND JUST ENJOY IT.

3 Dance

Put on a great song and
dance in your home.

Risky business it down the hallway in your socks or 'flash dance' it in your leg warmers. Just do what feels good.

SONG IDEAS

Anything by Beyonce, Madonna or Prince will
    get you up on your feet!
'Pour Some Sugar On Me' – Def Leppard
'Dancing With Myself' – Billy Idol
'Hit Me Baby One More Time' – Britney Spears
'Gimme, Gimme, Gimme' – ABBA

4
Do something kind

Compliment someone, tell someone you love them, bake something delicious and give it away or just scoff it yourself.

Most of all be kind to yourself, watch how you talk to yourself in your own head. Be careful not to say mean things. You don't deserve it, you really don't. Remember that a snake bite doesn't kill you, it's the venom that does.

5 Turn down the noise

Switch off your phone, TV, car radio, computer. Hear yourself think and enjoy the silence.

Try to listen to your soul. That quiet voice that can almost not be heard when we are too much in our busy lives. The one that tells us to go left or right, the one we ignore so often until it is too late and we have ended up in a dead end street for the millionth time.

6 Stretch

Reach as high as you can in the sky and then bend over and touch your toes or shins or whatever you can reach. Do some yoga poses, calf stretches or some cat stretches, it helps the energy move around your body and releases tension.

When we stretch our muscles we release stress and past traumas that are trapped and stored in our fascia/fat cells.

A really great practice is Qi-gong (pronounced Cheegoong) – there are amazing five-minute videos on YouTube that you can follow along to. Qi-gong is literally translated as 'energy work' and it's brilliant for getting the chi moving around your body. It's also a super chill and not at all strenuous exercise for those of us that are lazy. Ahem.

DID YOU KNOW THAT SORE BACKS AND NECKS ARE A DIRECT RESPONSE TO TRAUMAS THE BODY HAS EXPERIENCED IN THE PAST?

7 Crystals

Crystals have the ability to absorb and hold unique energies both positive and negative.

If you want to feel love put a rose quartz in your pocket or someplace so it's close to your heart.

If you're going to be around someone who is punishing, put a black stone in your pocket to absorb the negativity, and if you want some luck, grab a jade stone coupled with a citrine and perhaps a little quartz to action it.

You can throw some in your bath to charge the water too. Some combinations include:
Luck – jade, citrine and quartz
Love – rose quartz
Protection – amethyst and smoky quartz

REMEMBER TO CLEANSE YOUR CRYSTALS REGULARLY USING EITHER SAGE OR INCENSE SMOKE. OR YOU CAN PUT THEM IN A CUP OF WATER AND LEAVE OUTSIDE OVERNIGHT ON THE FULL MOON.

Smoky Quartz

Great stone for protecting yourself from negative energies. Smoky quartz also helps us break through stagnant energy.

Green Aventurine

The perfect stone for overcoming self-doubt while increasing self-worth.

Clear Quartz

This stone has a strong healing vibration. Clear quartz helps to stimulate the chakras as well as eliminating energy blockages. Clear quartz can also be used to charge other stones and amplify their frequencies.

Lapis Lazuli

This stone helps with wisdom and self-expression. The Egyptians used this stone for strength, clarity and confidence for its user.

Selenite

Has a heavenly connection to the divine. It carries a very strong vibration of love, light and truth.

Pet a cat

Any cat will do – even better, cuddle a purring cat on your chest. Purring raises your vibration and when you pat the cat the vibration is amplified again and again.

FAMILIARS ARE SMALL HOUSEHOLD PETS THAT SERVE AS A WITCH'S COMPANION. ACCORDING TO LEGEND THEY SERVE AS GUIDES WHO TAKE THE FORM OF AN ANIMAL ON EARTH. THEY ARE PROTECTORS TO WITCHES AND ASSIST IN THEIR MAGIC.

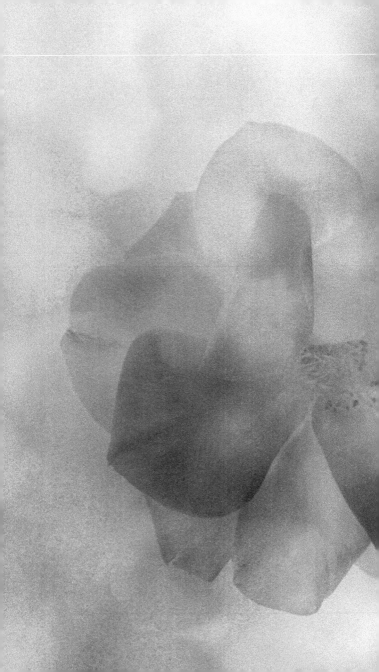

9 Smell rose oil

There is something truly spiritual and loving about the smell of rose oil or anything rose-scented.

If you need an extra bit of love, put a few drops on your wrists when you wake up. You can also steep rose petal tea, it smells like Chanel and tastes like heaven in a tea cup.

ROSE TEA

◇

Ingredients

1 tablespoon rose petals

Juice of half a lemon

2 cups water

Honey

Method

Bring to the boil all the ingredients except the honey on the stove top in your cauldron or just a regular pot. As you stir cast your intention into the tea.

Remove from the stove and add honey to taste. It should look pinkalicious!

IF YOU PUT SOME DROPS OF ESSENTIAL OIL ON THE CARDBOARD PART OF YOUR LOO ROLL YOUR BATHROOM WILL SMELL BEAUTIFUL ALL DAY.

10

Sage yourself

Burn a bundle of dried sage or a sage stick. This is called smudging and it is fab for banishing negative energy. Perfect after someone draining has been in your home or at the end of a long day.

You can also buy a sage spray if the 'pot' smell puts you off (or triggers your neighbours into calling the cops). It is also handy when travelling to clear any residual energy from other people, especially in hotel rooms.

Don't forget to spray the palms of your hands and the soles of your feet and the crown of your head!

DID YOU KNOW SAGE CAN CLEAR
94 PER CENT OF AIRBORNE BACTERIA?

HOW TO SMUDGE YOUR HOUSE

Light your stick and carry with you a bowl or dish to collect any falling debris. Begin at your front door and move the stick in clockwise circles, concentrating on windows and doors as they are the entry points to your home.

Be sure to allow the smoke to drift into corners and dark spaces (you can use a feather to encourage the smoke into place). When you are finished extinguish your stick in a bowl of salt or sand so you can reuse it.

Open windows an hour after you have finished smudging your house to allow the energy to exit.

11

Drink water

Chug a huge glass of water first thing in the morning. The body basically self-cleanses all night long and does a huge job of detoxifying itself, so reward it with something healthy instead of coffee, tea or juice.

Water not only hydrates but also cleanses and purifies the body. Enough said.

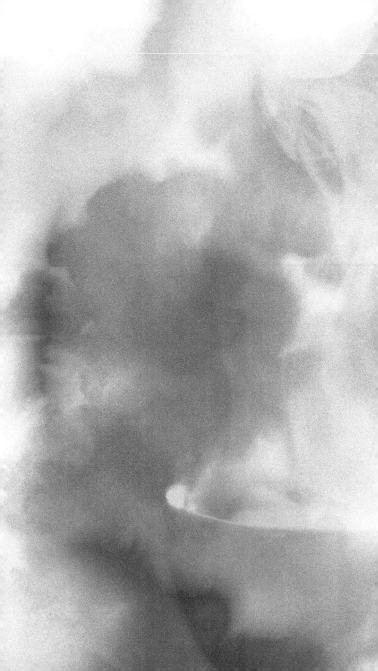

12

Herbal tea

According to Chinese medicine, fear and low-vibration energy live in the kidneys.

They say in TCM (Traditional Chinese Medicine) that you need to keep your kidneys warm in order to be able to manifest your dreams, and the best way to do that is with herbal teas. Kukicha is the best for calming the nervous system down.

You can also make 'herb simples' by adding a bunch of herbs to a hot glass of water and let it steep. Mugwort tea is an especially potent blend that can give you lucid dreams and induce astral travel, but don't drink it if you're pregnant or breastfeeding as it can start menstruation.

INTENTION TEA

◇

Brew yourself a cup of mugwort tea, let it steep for a few minutes and then sip slowly while journaling about where you need guidance.

Let the tea start to work and the drowsiness set in, remember to write down any symbols, numbers, colours or themes that were prevalent in your dreams and check in a dream dictionary. Auntyflo.com is a great site that deciphers the meaning of dreams.

13 Nature

Get out into nature.

Go to the park, mountains, the sea. Leave
your house and walk down the road. Get
out of your environment and see something
different. Walk barefoot on the beach, take
your shoes off and pad through the grass, sit
under a tree and dream. Dive in the water, or
even just dip your feet in.

14

Beauty

Look at something beautiful.

Go to an art gallery, watch kids play, walk
through a park, look at flowers, look at
beautiful homes, cars, jewellery, people,
clothing. Admire beauty in all its forms.

IF YOU CAN'T GET OUTSIDE GO ON TO
YOUTUBE AND SEARCH FOR 'BEAUTIFUL
NATURE SCENES OR IMAGES'. THERE ARE SO
MANY AWE-INSPIRING CLIPS AVAILABLE.

15

Sky

Lie on your back and look at the sky.

As the sun sets, sit or lie somewhere to look at the clouds. Witches call it skrying and say you can tell the future by the shapes the clouds form.

It's a super-relaxing thing to do and the sky is so beautiful at that time of day. It is also a wonderful moment to give thanks and gratitude for everything that is positive in your life.

MAKE IT A RITUAL BY POURING YOURSELF AN INTENTION TEA AND LIGHTING A CANDLE AND SOME INCENSE – THIS WAY YOU HAVE CREATED SACRED SPACE FOR YOURSELF.

16

Music

Play music while you cook.

The combination of chopping or mixing to beautiful music is incredibly relaxing, almost meditative. If you have had a stressful day this is a really lovely way to wind down. Whether it's classical music, movie soundtracks, jazz, rock 'n' roll, reggae, soul or funk, whatever blows your hair back.

SOME TV CHEFS EVEN HAVE A COMPILATION ON SPOTIFY THAT YOU CAN DOWNLOAD.

17

Choices

*It all matters. Even if
you just buy less and
slowly replace your
things with brands with
more integrity, this
works towards a higher
vibration of love.*

Choose with integrity.

Look at where your things are made and by whom.
Start aligning yourself with brands and products that
stand for your belief system. The vibration of quality,
cruelty-free, artisanal or organic products and produce
is high while anything mass-made, tested on animals,
under-paid or produced with child labour is low.

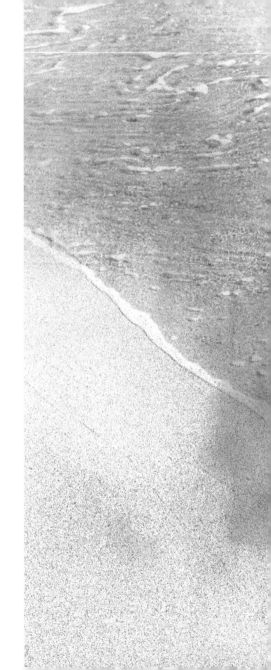

18

Say Ommmm

Say Ommm three times. Loudly.

The sound is the perfect vibration to balance and
raise vibration in your body.

To make the sound *ommm* is to ground and reconnect
with the earth. It is sound healing.

DID YOU KNOW THAT IF YOU OMMM AROUND
TINY BABIES THEY STOP CRYING?

19 Fresh flowers

Buy fresh flowers and plants.

Put two stems of something that lasts ages in a glass in your bathroom or next to your bed. Change the water every day and talk to your flowers – it really does work to keep them alive for longer.

Even just walking down the street, if you happen upon some jasmine or rosemary in someone's garden, stop and inhale their fragrance. It really is mood-altering. We live amongst so much beauty.

NATIVE FLOWERS LOOK BEAUTIFUL WHEN THEY ARE DRIED AND KEEP FOR AGES. IN EUROPE THEY CALL DRIED FLOWERS 'WINTER FLOWERS' AND KEEP THEM FOR THE WHOLE SEASON RATHER THAN THROWING THEM OUT.

20

Create an altar

An altar is a portal between this world, what witches call the mundane world, and the spiritual world. It reminds us that we are not just our physical bodies, but spiritual beings with infinite power to create what we want in our lives, and to feel connected to the divine when we feel lost or disconnected.

You can make one almost anywhere, but it is best to put it somewhere private so when you are doing your prayers or devotionals you won't be disturbed.

You can use crystals, shells, sand, special objects, coins, feathers and flowers to decorate yours. Or you can place a bowl of water facing west, a candle (fire) facing south, incense (air) facing east and a bowl of salt (earth) facing north in honour of the elements.

The idea is to give thanks and create an intention or purpose for the day. It also raises your vibration so you're in sync with the universe and can receive divine messages more easily.

Begin by grounding and thanking the elements by saying:
'Creature of air, I cleanse and consecrate thee in the name of the ancient energies of the east. Intuition and intellect I call to me!'

'Creature of fire, I cleanse and consecrate thee in the name of the ancient energies of the south. Passion and creativity I call to me!'

'Creature of water, I cleanse and consecrate thee in the name of the ancient energies of the west. Rebirth and transformation I call to me!'

'Creature of earth, I cleanse and consecrate thee in the name of the ancient energies of the north. Energy and stability I call to me!'

REMEMBER TO START YOUR DEVOTIONAL IN THE EAST (WITCHES ALWAYS START IN THE EAST!)

21

Slow down

Do one thing at a time. Go down three gears and concentrate on what is in front of you.

Just really listening to the person talking to you is a good start. Showing someone love is giving them your absolute presence.

Stop multi-tasking. Finish the thing you're doing before doing another thing.

DID YOU KNOW MOVING FASTER DOES NOT RAISE VIBRATION, BUT MOVING SLOWER DOES?

Jump up and down with your hands in the air like you just don't care.

22

jump

All that energy will move around your body and get you feeling much better.

1. Tense up your entire body as tight as you can and then release it.
2. Do jumping jacks for one minute.
3. Shake out your hands, wrists, arms, legs and booty. Twerk it a few times for good measure.
4. Stand still and feel the energy run through your body.

This is a great way to reset if you have been sitting still for too long and you need a jolt of energy. It's also an excellent remedy for taking you out of your head and into your body to silence the chatter.

23

Give gratitude

Say out loud three things that you're grateful for. Really simple but so effective.

You could make a list in your phone of stuff you love as a reminder:

Fresh bed sheets

The smell of baked bread or cookies or coffee

Hearing a cat purr

Warm towels out of the dryer

Baths

Chocolate-covered liquorice

The sound of cicadas

Diving into crystal clear water

Rainbows

Sun showers

24 Uplifting people

Being around uplifting people is easier said than done, right? It may not feel like you can connect to people around you sometimes, but keep searching for your tribe.

Don't stop until you find them. You will know when you find them because they will bring out the magic in you and not the madness.

Concentrate on uplifting your own energy and practising the exercises in this book and naturally you will attract like-minded people. Like attracts like, so keep your side of the street clean and have good spiritual hygiene.

25

Tibetan singing bowls

◇
◆

These bowls are used for sound healing by Tibetan monks in spiritual ceremonies.

Singing bowls can generate 'theta' waves in your brain. This is great for manifesting, deep relaxation, creativity and problem solving as well as subconscious training to bring you into the here and now.

They reduce stress and anxiety, lower blood pressure, improve blood circulation, increase mental clarity, stimulate the immune system and promote positive energy. Phew!

YOU DON'T HAVE TO BUY ONE, YOU CAN FIND 'TIBETAN SINGING BOWL' MEDITATION CLIPS ON YOUTUBE.

YOUR BRAIN OPERATES ON
FIVE MAIN FREQUENCIES

Beta

We live in beta 95 per cent of our waking hours
and it is the logical part of our brain.

Alpha

The state you are in during mediation where you
feel 'in flow' with the universe.

Theta

When you are at your most creative and feel
open and guided. This is the best state for
visualisation and manifestation.

Delta

The sleep state.

Gamma

Is a state of being that is very rare, mainly found
by monks.

26

Light incense

Create a ritual (how I love a ritual!)
of lighting incense first thing
when you wake up.

If you're feeling deep and spiritual, burn nag champa.
Burn rose if you want more love (always!).
White sage if you need cleansing.
Dragon's blood if you're feeling witchy.

Use a charcoal disk and resin incense for spells. Place
a few pebbles of copal or frankincense/myrrh to
create some drama and get you in the mood.

FRANKINCENSE/MYRRH IS A REALLY POWERFUL
INCENSE. USE LITTLE TONGS TO HANDLE THE
RED HOT DISK AND SIT IT IN A MINI CAULDRON.
I KNOW, I KNOW, A CAULDRON, HILARIOUS. BUT
REALLY, EVERY HOUSE SHOULD HAVE ONE.

27

Laugh

Out loud, preferably.

Watch something funny, do something funny, wear something funny. Just find the humour.

DID YOU KNOW THAT LAUGHING SWAPS CORTISOL IN OUR BLOODSTREAM WITH DOPAMINE, OXYTOCIN AND ENDORPHINS?

28

Sing

In the car, in the house, do it in the street if you have the guts.

Car jamming is the nightclub of 2022. It doesn't matter if you have the world's worst voice, who cares, nobody can hear you anyway!

IF YOU HAVEN'T BEEN KARAOKE-ING IN THE LAST DECADE YOU SERIOUSLY NEED TO DO IT. LIKE NOW.

29 Feel your feelings

Lie down and ask yourself how you feel. Wait for the feeling to surface and greet it like a friend.

Let it sit with you a while and listen to it. Even the yucky feelings need to be heard. We push them away so much because we are scared of them, but they are just like people; they need to be heard and acknowledged.

When you first start practising this exercise sadness may come up. That's OK. Don't push away sadness or anger or any of the other emotions; give them a time and a place to be heard. Let it hurt.

FEELING EXERCISE

Ask yourself, 'How do I feel?' Let the feeling come up. Don't judge it, just sit with the feeling until it passes.

30

I love you

Tell someone you love them.

Even if it's your cat. Also, tell yourself in the
mirror and while you're at it, tell yourself
'I am good enough.' This will feel super-
uncomfortable at first, but keep doing it until
it doesn't and you can say, 'Hell yeah I am!'

31

Wear pink

◇
◆

Pink is the colour of love and is typically associated with feminine energy. It also corresponds with the heart chakra.

WHAT ARE CHAKRAS?

◇

Chakra is Sanskrit for spinning wheel or vortex.
In eastern spiritual traditions, they believe that we
have seven main chakras aligned from the base of
our spine to the top of our heads. Each colour has
its own frequency vibration and corresponds to a
particular chakra (or energy centre) in your body.

Selecting the right colour when you get dressed
in the morning helps you to harness its frequency
vibration, so you create intention in your world.

Root – (base of the spine) Red
Sacrel – (stomach) Orange
Solar – (chest) Yellow
Heart – Green (or sometimes Pink)
Throat – Blue
Third eye – Violet
Crown – White Light

Did you know that violet is the highest
vibrational colour? In fact, its energy is so
high it can burn our skin very quickly and
kill bacteria.

32 Healthy food

Eat something fresh and healthy

Raw fruit and veggies have the highest vibration. Things like green leafy veggies, lettuce, kale, arugula, collard greens, chard and sprouts are literally akin to eating the energy of the sun.

The cleaner and less modified the food, the higher the energetic vibration. Basically it's all about the food being alive or living and not dead. You want lots of healthy enzymes in your body so you can feel your best.

WITCHY GREEN SHAKE FOR GLOWY SKIN

Ingredients

2 cups rice or almond milk

A frozen banana

1 tablespoon protein powder
   (I use Sun Warrior in vanilla)

1 tablespoon carob powder

1 tablespoon cocoa powder

1 teaspoon bee pollen

1 tablespoon flaxseed oil

1 tablespoon spirulina
   (I use two, but I'm a bit of a freak with it)

Method

Blend on high for two minutes.

33

Lie in the sun

Let those rays kiss your skin for a while. Bask like a cat in a patch of sunshine. I promise you really will purr.

Just in case you needed proof, the health benefits of sunlight include:

Stress reduction
Strengthens your bones
Boosts your immune system
Fights off depression
Improves your sleep
Elevates your mood
Can give you a longer life

DID YOU KNOW THAT MODERATE SUNLIGHT EXPOSURE BOOSTS SEROTONIN (THE HAPPINESS HORMONE) LEVELS IN YOUR BODY?

Just like sunbathing, except at night. It may sound weird, but we get energised by the moon. Remember the average human body is up to 60 per cent water.

If the tides are affected by the moon, then we most certainly are.

Moonbathing is an ancient Ayurvedic ritual that has many benefits, including cooling and calming inflammation in the body.

If you can, lie outside and expose as much of your skin to the moonlight. Enhance it even more by surrounding yourself with bowls of water, which you can later use to drink or bathe in. If it's freezing or you don't want nosy neighbours to think you're a weirdo, lie somewhere with the blinds open. Read a book or chill out with the moon in view.

MOONBATHING IS BEST DONE BETWEEN THE NEW MOON AND THE FULL MOON. ACCORDING TO WITCHES THIS IS ALSO THE MOST EFFECTIVE TIME TO SET INTENTIONS.

35

Tidy up

A wise witch I know once said to me, 'When you feel your worst, look your best.'

Use all your best creams and lotions, wash your hair, groom and smother yourself in sweet-smelling things then change into something you love.

If you can, use natural oils and soaps on your skin and hair. Our skin is our largest organ and everything we put on it goes directly into our bloodstream. Intuitively it makes sense that we should only put natural things on it.

36

Clean your space

*This is why witches
have broomsticks.*

When you create a magical or high-vibration
space, you must clean it first to get rid of any
stagnation or bad energy.

37

Chuck stuff out ———

Things are charged with energy too.

The best way to shift energy and invite a higher vibration into your home is to chuck stuff out. Start with your bathroom and then head under your kitchen sink.

If you haven't used it in six months, bin it or give it away. As Elsa from *Frozen* said, 'Let it go! Let it go!'

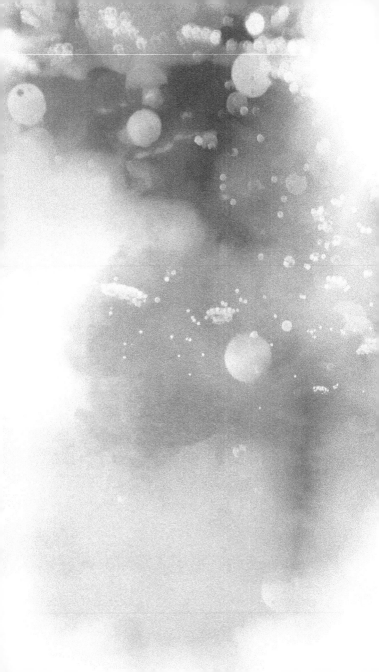

38

Take a nap

Sometimes when you're feeling overwhelmed, it's best just to go back to bed.

Even if it's for a 20-minute snooze on the couch or in your chair. From time to time, your body needs to reboot like a computer.

DID YOU KNOW A QUICK DISCO NAP IN THE MIDDLE OF THE DAY CAN IMPROVE YOUR MOOD, MEMORY, JOB PERFORMANCE, EASE STRESS AND MAKE YOU MORE ALERT?

39

Be generous

Give without expectation.
Give stuff, give time, give energy,
give thanks. Give it away.

Make up a box of treats and send it to people in the post. Think of the people you love and who would appreciate it most.

SHIFT YOUR THINKING OF WHAT CAN I DO FOR ME TO WHAT CAN I DO FOR SOMEONE ELSE.

Meditation

Find thousands of mini high-vibration meditations on YouTube.

Find a comfy place to sit cross-legged (the couch is perfect). Keep a straight spine so your chakras are aligned and energy can flow freely through your body, and listen to the hypnotic voice or music.

After you have finished the meditation it is the optimal time to visualise as your brain is in a theta state. This is THE secret to manifesting.

I LIKE CHAKRA-BALANCING MEDITATIONS AND TIBETAN BOWL MUSIC BUT YOU CAN JUST SEARCH 'HIGH VIBE MEDITATIONS'.

41

Journaling

Write down all your feelings without censorship.

It's a really great way to get thoughts out of your head and on to paper. When you read back through the days, you begin to see how quickly we cycle through feelings. A lot will have passed and probably quicker than you thought.

MAKE SURE YOU HIDE THE BOOK SOMEWHERE VERY GOOD, OR EVEN BETTER, PUT IT IN YOUR PHONE NOTES WHERE YOU HAVE A SECURITY PIN.

42

Send love

◇

◆

Send love to someone who needs it. Add this on to the end of your mediation or you can do it any time you think of it really.

*Firstly, open your heart chakra by
thinking of the things you love.
People, pets, places, food – anything
that causes you to smile.*

Next, sigh very loudly and smile. Just these simple
things will open your heart chakra up wide. Now
think about the person you want to send love to and
imagine green glowing energy flowing from your
heart towards them and bathing them in its light.
Sometimes I do this after I read about an upsetting
situation in the world that I want to heal.

Louise Hay said that you should always send love
ahead of you, even if it's to the coffee shop you go to
in the morning before you get there.

I swear this works: every day the girl behind the
counter randomly draws a love heart on my cup!

43

Hugging

Give someone a really long hug! For at least 20 seconds.

We have a biological need for human touch. When you touch the skin it stimulates pressure sensors under the skin that send messages to the vagus (a nerve in the brain).

As vagal activity increases, the nervous system slows down, heart rate and blood pressure decrease and brain waves show relaxation. After 20 seconds, the bonding hormone oxytocin is released. This hormone is said to lower blood pressure and improve your mood.

44

Passion

Follow your passion.

Read, learn, listen to podcasts; totally immerse yourself in your passion. The intensity of passion is in itself a high vibration. The more we stay in the passion, the higher our vibration will be.

Passion gives us purpose!

45

Create something

Put something into the world
that nobody else has before.

Even if it's just a poem or a drawing or an idea, it matters. It all goes to create a higher vibration for the planet.

46

Morning ritual

◈

Cultivate a morning routine. Watch the sunrise, meditate and make yourself a cup of green tea. Give yourself some time to wake up properly and set intentions for the day.

Rushing in the mornings is low vibe. Be protective of your morning routine, create that sacred space, the time that is just for you.

1. Shower first thing.
2. Body brush.
3. Drink a glass of hot water with half a lemon in it.
4. Light incense.
5. Say into the mirror 'I love you [insert name]'.
6. Raise your vibration through meditation. When your vibration is nice and high you can do a five-minute (or longer) visualisation of what you would like to manifest into your life.
7. Do 20–40 mins yoga if you can. Otherwise a five-minute stretch is fine too.

GET UP EARLIER THAN PARTNERS, PARENTS OR SIBLINGS, SO THEY LEAVE YOU ALONE.

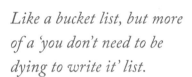

47

F#@$ it list

Like a bucket list, but more of a 'you don't need to be dying to write it' list.

Write down all the things you would do in your life if you just thought 'F#@$ it.'

Things like:
Start a band
Sing on stage
Learn to dance the tango
Sculpt
Live in NYC for a year
Go on a silent retreat

48

Digital declutter

*Delete old numbers and
photos on your phone.*

When you delete the old you make space for
new people and experiences to enter your
life. A perfect way to close a chapter and
open a new one.

Stop hoarding numbers and memories,
create new ones!

49

Tell the truth

Telling the truth leads to revolution
both for yourself and the planet.

Historically speaking the world doesn't really like a
truth teller. However, I have learnt the hard way that
telling the truth is the only way, even if it hurts.

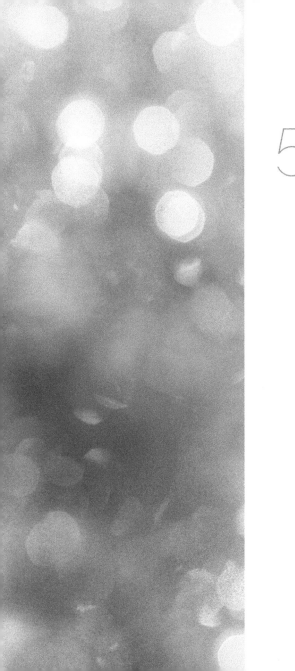

50

Mirror work

Old-school Louise Hay-style mirror work. After 30 years this stuff is still revolutionary.

One fine morning I realised that all I had to do to change the image I had of myself was to change my mind. I started looking in the mirror and saying, 'I approve of myself'. I turned every angle of myself in the nude and said to every inch of me (under downlighting no less) 'I love you, Jade. I see your cellulite and I love you. I see you, back fat and I love you too. I love your cute, soft, pudgy skin!'

*That is the beginning of learning
to love and accept yourself.*

The beginning I said! The rest is hard.

Real life obstructs our best intentions to love
ourselves. We may have a bad night's sleep and the
next day beat ourselves up mentally. We may have a
friend or family member who likes to project their
own weird body image on to us.

So, in order to remedy that, you must really believe
and practise affirmations. Say them enough times
a day so that you really truly own them. When you
do this, a miracle will happen. Those people, the
ones that support your crappy self-image, they will
disappear (or at least their commentary will). You
will glow from the inside out and people around you
will notice. You may from time to time encounter the
odd jab, but nothing you can't deal with because you
know they are wrong.

*You are love itself, beautiful, unique,
strong, sexy, sumptuous love in
form. Your own unique form.*

Introductory spells ———

◇
◆

Create sacred space by smudging the room in which you will perform the ritual and then ground and centre.

A SPELL FOR RELEASE

This spell is wonderful for releasing grief and attachment to low-vibration feelings like guilt, shame, anger and hurt.

1. Go into the ocean and submerge yourself from head to toe.
2. Let seven small waves crash over you.
3. Each time say out loud, 'I give my tears to the tide and let it take them out to sea, please take this negative energy far away from me.'

MOON WATER

Fill a glass jug or bottle with filtered water and place outside on the full moon. Put a sticky label on the outside with what star sign the moon is in.

You can use an app like The Moon to tell you the phases and signs. Each star sign carries certain characteristics that you can use in your spell work.

LOVE SPELL

Ingredients

Red paper cut into a heart shape

Pen

Seven pearl-tipped pins

A candle

Smudge stick

A mirror

This spell is performed on the night of the full moon for seven nights consecutively. It must be performed 'skyclad' (that is witch-speak for naked).

Create sacred space by smudging the room in which you will perform the ritual and then ground and centre.

Method

1. Stand in front of the mirror naked and light your candle.
2. Write on the red heart all the qualities you would like in a partner – be specific and use front and back if you want.
3. Stare at yourself in the mirror and read your heart out loud and pierce the heart with the pin. Visualise your heart filling with a pink light.
4. Repeat every night for seven nights and let the candle burn for seven minutes each time.

READ THE QUALITIES ON THE RED HEART OFTEN TO YOURSELF. TRY TO BE ALL THE THINGS YOU WANT IN SOMEONE ELSE. LIKE ATTRACTS LIKE. THE MORE WHOLE YOU ARE YOURSELF AS A PERSON THE MORE POWERFULLY YOU WILL MANIFEST THIS IN A PARTNER.

Did you know that as new illnesses appear herbalists are finding more and more new species of plants that help with that particular complaint? Nature is so magical.

SELF-LOVE JAR

Ingredients

Himalayan salt

A handful of rose petals

A pinch of cinnamon (for passion and love and to
speed up the spell)

1 teaspoon of sugar or honey (to attract)

A note to yourself saying, 'I love you [insert name]'

Seal with wax (red for love)

A small glass jar with a cork or lid

Method

Witchcraft is about intention. While you are
preparing your jar, concentrate on your energy going
into it, meditate on what you would like to achieve as
you place each ingredient into the jar.

Ingredients

A handful of chamomile

1 cinnamon stick

A pinch of basil

A splash of water

1 green birthday candle

1 sheet of paper

Method

1. Pour water into a bowl with a handful of chamomile leaves, mix with your hands and rub into your hands for increased luck.

2. In a mortar and pestle mix together the basil, cinnamon and chamomile.

3. Meditate while you mix and visualise coins running through your hands as you hold your hands over the bowl.

4. Write out a note with the exact amount you wish to attract and by which date five times and sign it.

5. Fill a jar with the mixture.

6. Coat a green birthday candle with the herbal mix and burn one end so it sticks to the top of the jar, let it melt to seal the jar and say an enchantment and end by saying, 'So mote it be.'

Ingredients

Holy basil (tulsi)

Rhodiola

Ashwagandha

Method

Add 1 teaspoon of each herb into a mug and let steep for a few minutes, strain and then drink.

This combination is the holy trinity of adaptogens. It centres, grounds, calms and opens the heart chakra.

WHAT ARE ADAPTOGENS? THEY ARE NON-TOXIC PLANTS THAT HELP THE BODY RESIST STRESSORS OF ALL KINDS, WHETHER PHYSICAL, CHEMICAL OR BIOLOGICAL. USED FOR CENTURIES IN AYURVEDIC AND CHINESE HEALING TRADITIONS, THEY ARE HAVING A RENAISSANCE TODAY.

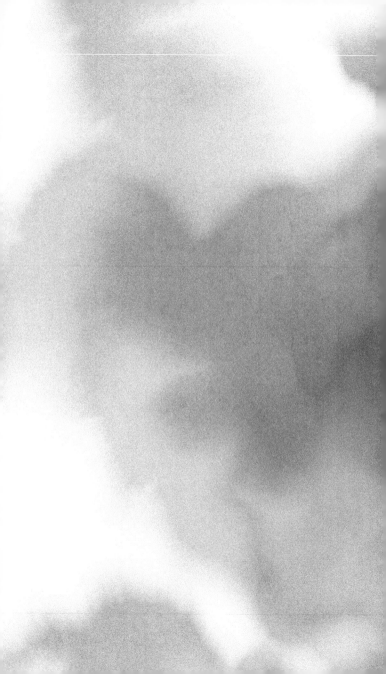

BTW, if I have contradicted myself in any way, or acted like I know it all, that is part of the process. We are all just trying to figure it out as we go.

IN CLOSING

*It all begins and ends with you.
Do not put your opinion of yourself
in someone else's hands. Take back
your power by loving yourself.*

What I came to find during my own journey was
that I am simply me, doing my very best every day,
just trying to show up for myself and not betray
myself. I am flawed and a bit unravelled and still a
bit raw.

Each time life punches me in the guts I know I have
only me to rely on to pull myself up off my knees.

I still struggle with swearing (a very hard habit to
break) and I have been known to eat a packet of
chocolate biscuits for dinner and binge-watch reality
television. Basically, I don't like to be hard and fast
on rules in general.

I have never liked authority and especially dislike
being told what to do. Even by myself. So please
forgive me if anything I write sounds militant,
inflexible or smug.

Don't give up hope. Know that the pain will ease and this too shall pass and your beautiful resilient little heart will learn to love again. But first it must love you. It is time to do the work.

Grief is not like sleeping off a hangover. You have to be present in your own healing, and it is a long road with many winding trails, sharp corners and sheer inclines.

Remember, it doesn't matter how you get there, as long as you get there.

Maybe we need to change our idea of love. See it as inner before outer. When you have empathy and love for yourself, you have empathy and love for others.

*Our heart doesn't
beat for someone else,
it beats for us!*